When Lucifer and Jezebel
Join Your Church

Dick Bernal

Scripture quotations are from the Holy Bible, New King James Version, copyright 1991 by Thomas Nelson, Inc.

Front cover design: Jorge Boas Design
Back cover design: Erin Gilman
Editing, layout and page makeup: Lynda Johnson

ISBN 1–884920–00–4

Published by
Jubilee Christian Center
175 Nortech Parkway
San Jose, California 95134

Printed by
Patson's Press
Sunnyvale, California
USA

Second Printing, July 1995

CONTENTS

QUOTABLE QUOTES

Life is just a test. This is only a test.—Kevin Gerald

When you're going through hell, don't stop.—Mario Murillo

Never, never, never, never quit.—Sir Winston Churchill

And this too shall pass.—Melva Lea

*The word 'crisis' in the Chinese language means
'danger' or 'opportunity.'*—Peter J. Daniels

*I don't mind being in the furnace if Jesus
is in there with me.*—Larry Lea

*Nothing happens to you that hasn't happened
to someone else.*—William Feather

*The ocean keeps itself clean
by constant agitation.*—Dr. David Cho

The brook would lose its song without the rocks.—Anonymous

*The existence of the sea means
the existence of pirates.*—Old Malay Proverb

Honey, why don't you just do what you preach?—Carla Bernal

INTRODUCTION

I said, "Lord, be merciful to me; heal my soul, for I have sinned against You." My enemies speak evil of me: "When will he die, and his name perish?" And if he comes to see me, he speaks lies; his heart gathers iniquity to itself; when he goes out, he tells it.

All who hate me whisper together against me; against me they devise my hurt. "An evil disease," they say, "clings to him. And now that he lies down, he will rise up no more." Even my own familiar friend in whom I trusted, who ate my bread, has lifted up his heel against me.

Psalm 41:4-9

Can you relate to David? You're a leader in God's kingdom. You're not perfect. Like all of us, you've made a mistake or two, but you repent, correct the problem and keep on keeping on. But out of seemingly nowhere comes a rebellion within the leadership ranks. An associate, perhaps an elder, someone close to you turns on you and gets others to do the same. Before you know it, you have a split on your hands. What happened? Where did you miss it? Could it have been prevented?

This little book may have the answer for you and save you future heartache. We are going to look at the two most dangerous spirits in our churches today: Lucifer and Jezebel. This is a shocking exposure of Satan's tactics to diffuse the power of leadership.

Chapter 1

CLIMBERS
IN LEADERSHIP

After thirteen years of pioneering one church in one city and seeing staff come and go, I feel somewhat qualified to address this subject. I've had more than one associate and elder go south on me.

Had I listened to my wife, I never would have hired or appointed them in the first place, but I'm a slow learner so I've been burned a few times. Like most pastors, I love and trust everyone. My wife discerns behind the scenes. I used to think she was hyper-critical, and boy, did we have more than one lively debate over some of my decisions about who was appointed what position and when.

Being an impetuous visionary of a 6000-member church, I tended to look for the gifted, talented and excited sort. Carla looked for integrity, loyalty, tithing track record and character. She now helps in the interviewing of potential staff and her opinion is taken to heart.

In reading this book I might sound a little harsh. "Sour grapes" one might say. Well, let me begin by accepting my responsibility in letting the wrong people get into leadership. The first finger to be pointed must be pointed at me. So be it!

As I approach 50, I'm getting not only older, but smarter. And to tell you the truth, persecution is good for the soul. Fruit is grown in the valley, not on the mountain tops.

Let's turn our mistakes and setbacks into victories and take heart—the Bible is full of like situations. God had his "church" split by Lucifer; Adam and Eve had a family split by a son named Cain; Noah had Ham and Canaan; Joseph had his brothers; Moses had Aaron, Miriam and Korah; Joshua had Achan; Samson had Delilah; David had Saul and Absalom; Esther and Mordecai had Haman; Elijah had Jezebel; Jesus had Judas; and Paul had Alexander, the coppersmith.

Great leaders come under great attack. Recently I ran into a former church member who was backslidden and as they say, "down and out." I bought him lunch, a room for a couple of nights at a local motel and encouraged him in the Lord. At lunch he asked me what horrible thing I had done to a couple who were mutual friends of ours and leaders in our church.

"Nothing that I know of," I assured him. "Well, boy Pastor, they sure have it in for you," he related. "You should hear the things they're saying about you and Carla.

"Pastor," he continued, "not long ago I slept with a prostitute and I felt so convicted! I begged God to forgive me and then I took a two-hour shower to wash the filth off me. You know, I felt the same after I talked with that couple. I felt so filthy; I took a long shower and repented for allowing myself to be a garbage can for their trash."

Interesting, here's a man who's backslidden and for the most part out of fellowship with God. Yet he still has enough discernment to recognize the working of unclean spirits.

I went to this couple somewhat perplexed. They were embarrassed to meet with me. They are really nice people who had been listening to other people. Once we sat down and began to talk, things got straightened out. Some of what they heard had truth to it. Most didn't.

Isn't it fascinating how we form an opinion about people by what others think and say? We repeat things as if it were gospel truth simply because we heard it through a "friend." As one pastor said, "We judge others on what we hear and what they do, but we judge ourselves on our good intentions." We defend no one more than our own precious selves.

Allowing others' feelings to become your feelings is really a form of spiritual rape. Have you ever been in a conversation about another leader in the body and know the conversation is going a direction you don't want it to go? You can feel a blinking yellow light inside warning you to be cautious, slow down, prepare to stop.

In the following chapters we will look at and identify cancer cells in leadership—cells that look to kill, destroy or cripple. Cells such as:
- Rebellion
- Control ✓
- Deception
- Manipulation
- Divisiveness
- Gossip ✓
- Sowers of discord
- Self-righteousness ✓
- Authority-hating

- Uncleanness
- Accusation ✓
- Lying ✓
- Power hungry
- Anger ✓
- Bitterness
- Jealousy ✓
- Ambition
- Fanaticism
- Super-spirituality ✓

And if I left a few out, you go ahead and write them in yourself.

Probably the most overlooked Scripture in all of holy writ is found in Galatians 6:7:

> *Do not be deceived, God is not mocked; for whatever a man sows, that he will also reap.*

If you and I really believed that, we like Job would put our hand over our mouth several times a day and pray for crop failure for junk we've sown in the past. Yet somehow we think we are going to be the first person in the whole universe to get away with sowing discord.

> *These six things the Lord hates, yes, seven are an abomination to Him: a proud look, a lying ton-gue, hands that shed innocent blood, a heart that devises wicked plans, feet that are swift in running to evil, a false witness who speaks lies, and one who sows discord among brethren.*
>
> Proverbs 6:16-19

I don't think this is just filler to thicken the Bible!

When I came out of Rhema Bible Training Center, I knew it all. I was a young, lean, Bible-quoting machine. My poor pastor had a mess on his hands. Pastor Vince was a former Roman Catholic priest who got Jesus, the Holy Ghost and new doctrine. But he didn't know what I knew, bless God, and I let a few church folks know about it now and then.

At the time I didn't think I was in rebellion, really! I thought I was simply going to change the whole church and make it what I thought it should be—you know, better. But what I was doing was causing problems. Let me stop here and defend my alma mater. My behavior was not promoted by the school as a way to win friends and influence God!

Pastor Vince was so kind and patient, even though all this zeal of mine was causing him grief. This gentle, fatherly man simply loved me in spite of my inflated opinion of my spirituality. I guess he knew that someday as a pastor I would get the same treatment from my own "climbers," but he didn't tell me I'd have three of them! God must really love me to allow me to reap such great returns...ouch!

All right, lesson learned. Let's move on.

Chapter 2

MODE
OF OPERATION

You could say the Jezebel spirit primarily works through women or effeminate men. The Lucifer spirit will attach itself in most cases to men.

Before the fall of mankind through Adam and Eve, Lucifer was in the inner circle of leadership. He was very religious, gifted, powerful, influential and strong-willed.

Lucifer means "light-bearer" or "star."

Jezebel in the Hebrew means, "Where is Baal?"

Both usurped authority.

Both were unhappy in subordinate roles.

Both were wily, scheming, opposing and deceptive.

These spirits are attracted to strong prophetic, charismatic, faith churches but are found to some degree in all Christian churches.

They will work through some of the nicest people you've ever met. Gifted, loyal, giving, praying, volunteering people who look like an answer to prayer, and they may be at first. But because of a character flaw, a wound that never healed or some other dysfunctional trait that was underground for a season, they are easy prey for these spirits. You won't pick up a potential problem unless your discerner is working.

Usually people with these spirits start the climb into leadership. They try to get real chummy with the pastor and his wife. They do and say all the right things. Again we must remember to heed Ephesians 6:16:

> *Above all, taking the shield of faith with which you will be able to quench all the fiery darts of the wicked one.*

In most cases the persons involved with these spirits are victims who are being used by the devil to victimize. Deception is a very strong force, not to be underestimated.

Here are some warning signs characteristic of people being used by the Lucifer and Jezebel spirits. They are people who:

- Look for authority without much responsibility.
- Always warn you about other leaders.
- Give special gifts to the pastor/spouse.
- Ask you to bend the rules for them every now and then.
- Start to have their own "following."
- Don't show up on Sunday if some big shot is preaching at another church.
- Give irregularly.
- Always have a "word" for you (a letter).
- Need constant attention.
- Want desperately to be an elder.

The most common places for these spirits to work are in home Bible studies, prayer groups, cliques or any other gathering place off church grounds.

16

This does not mean we shouldn't have home cell or care groups in our churches, but it does tell us to know what's going on and who is in leadership.

New converts can't and won't hurt you. They're just glad to be saved and accepted. It's the dissatisfied. The one who needs appreciation and attention. The church hopper who has "seen it all," "heard it all" and was "sent by God" to help you.

Be extremely cautious of people who tell you all that is wrong with their former church and pastor, and how they tried to help but no one would listen, so God led them out. Also be careful of the person God is always "talking to."

"Super spiritual" people are usually super flaky and can be a super problem!

Remember, all ministries have problems. We all miss it now and again. Some of the greatest preachers in the world have blundered, but what makes them great is how, with integrity, they handle their mistakes. God gives grace to the humble, but resists the proud. God in His Word does not just let us see the patriarchs and matriarchs of faith succeed, but He gives us a peek into their failures. This is to give us all hope that grace and mercy do indeed follow the upright.

Dr. C. M. Ward once told me, "Son, confess your sins to God and your faults to man." He went on to add, "Only God can truly forgive and forget. Man struggles in that area and as David said, 'Lord, against you and you only have I sinned.'"

David's dilemma in our introductory Scripture pas-sage (Psalm 41) is that his enemies, even former friends, were trying to use his mistakes to destroy him. God judges to deliver, but the spirits of Lucifer and Jezebel judge to condemn and destroy.

You can tell the truth about someone and still bring a curse on yourself if your motive is to hurt or discredit that individual. We will discuss this further later on.

Truth is a two-edged sword. Like a surgeon's knife, it can cut to heal or like an enemy's sword, it can cut to kill. Bear your soul to very few outside of your mate. There are those around you who will use it against you. I'm not being paranoid; I'm just sharing out of personal experience and that of hundreds of pastors I know. I've seen it happen over and over again. Our greatest strength, being transparent, open and honest, can be taken by some as a weakness or carnality. Choose your staff and friends with care and prayer.

Chapter 3

LUCIFER—
WHAT WENT WRONG?

Lucifer • Light Bearer • Son of the Morning

What caused this gifted and loyal associate—
Lucifer—to split the first church and lead a third of the
congregation into starting their own church?

How did his rebellion become their rebellion?

If we can locate the root of the problem, perhaps we
can eliminate this from ever happening in our churches.
Let's examine two familiar Scripture passages, one in
Ezekiel and the other in Isaiah:

> *Moreover the word of the Lord came to me,*
> *saying, "Son of man, take up a lamentation for the*
> *king of Tyre, and say to him, 'Thus says the Lord*
> *God: "You were the seal of perfection, full of*
> *wisdom and perfect in beauty. You were in Eden,*
> *the garden of God; every precious stone was your*
> *covering: The sardius, topaz, and diamond, beryl,*
> *onyx, and jas-per, sapphire, turquoise, and*
> *emerald with gold. The workmanship of your*
> *timbrels and pipes was prepared for you on the*
> *day you were created. You were the anointed*
> *cherub who covers; I established you; you were*
> *on the holy mountain of God; you walked back and*
> *forth in the midst of fiery stones. You were*

perfect in your ways from the day you were created, till iniquity was found in you.

"By the abundance of your trading you became filled with violence within, and you sinned; therefore I cast you as a profane thing out of the mountain of God; and I destroyed you, O covering cherub, from the midst of the fiery stones.

Pride ←   "Your heart was lifted up because of your beauty; you corrupted your wisdom for the sake of your splendor; I cast you to the ground, I laid you before kings, that they might gaze at you.

"You defiled your sanctuaries by the multitude of your iniquities, by the iniquity of your trading; therefore I brought fire from your midst; it devoured you, and I turned you to ashes upon the earth in the sight of all who saw you. All who knew you among the peoples are astonished at you; you have become a horror, and shall be no more forever."'"

Ezekiel 28:11-19

Hell from beneath is excited about you, to meet you at your coming; it stirs up the dead for you, all the chief ones of the earth; it has raised up from their thrones all the kings of the nations.

They all shall speak and say to you: "Have you also become as weak as we? Have you become like us? Your pomp is brought down to Sheol, and the sound of your stringed instruments; the maggot is spread under you, and worms cover you."

How you are fallen from heaven, O Lucifer, son of the morning! How you are cut down to the ground, you who weakened the nations! For you have said in your heart: "I will ascend into heaven, I will exalt my throne above the stars of God; I will also sit on the mount of the congregation on the farthest sides of the north; I will ascend above the heights of the clouds, I will be like the Most High." Yet you shall be brought down to Sheol, to the lowest depths of the Pit.

> *Those who see you will gaze at you, and*
> *consider you, saying: "Is this the man who made*
> *the earth tremble, who shook kingdoms, who made*
> *the world as a wilderness and destroyed its cities,*
> *who did not open the house of his prisoners?"*

Isaiah 14:9-17

First let's look at Ezekiel 28. Today we know Satan to be deceptive, cunning, wily, crafty, lying, accusing, clever, subtle, an angel of light and full of wrath. He is referred to as "serpent," "that old dragon" and "roaring lion seeking whom he may devour." But what of days gone by? Once he was a trusted loyal servant of God. Notice in verse 12 he's referred to as:

seal of perfection

wise

beautiful.

Verse 13 shows that he was unique; no other angel was like him. Not only was he wise and beautiful, but he was also musical. Notice the last part of verse 13, *On the day you were created*. We will talk more on this later.

In verse 14 we see that he had an anointing and much authority—*who covers*.

What an associate! Who wouldn't hire this guy? He's sharp, wise, good looking, charming, can administrate, teach and lead worship.

Proximity

Lucifer had great favor with God. Close in proximity to the Trinity, he walked with and talked with God.

Again, verse 15 tells us that he was *created*. He didn't just arrive on the scene under his own power. His

21

position on staff was created by the "Big Pastor Himself"
—God Almighty. Pastor, hear me! You are called. All
others are sent by God to help. Positions on staff are
created positions.

Recently we had a real tragedy in our church. I
won't go into detail, but a former assistant and friend is
no longer on staff for very good reasons. This man used
to say, "Jubilee would be nothing without me." My wife
Carla rebuked him one evening and told him only God
gets the credit for our church, not man, not even Dick
and Carla, the founders.

Our church was already eight years old when we
found this guy. He was broke, somewhat homeless and
had no car, but he did have obvious gifts and talents. I
created a position for him, hired him, and gave him a
good starting salary, enough to get a car and into a nice
home. Yet pride got to him. Like Lucifer he became
ungrateful and obviously bored with an assistant's role.

More than one pastor has shared similar stories
with me. "Why is it?" they ask. "The ones you love and
help the most are often the ones who turn on you the
quickest."

Spirit of Pride

Also in verse 15, we see that iniquity was found in
Lucifer. Verse 16 goes on to add, *by the abundance of
your trading* (trafficking). Notice the fruit of sin:

verse 16 • Violence
 • Profanity
 • Destruction
verse 17 • Pride
 • Corruption

verse 18 • Defilement

• Multitude of sin

verse 19 • Eternal horror

Let's again look at Isaiah chapter 14, starting with verse 12.

> *How you are fallen from heaven, O Lucifer, son of the morning! How you are cut down to the ground, you who weakened the nations!*

We know from Scripture that pride goes before a fall. Here's the biggest free-fall of all.

Lucifer had a bad case of the "*I wills.*" Notice verse 13, the first of the *I wills.*

1. *I will ascend into heaven.* Lucifer won't be satisfied with starting his own church. He wants God's. "Hey man, watch me. I'm taking over this place."

2. *I will exalt my throne above the stars of God.* Here we see self-righteousness and absurd deception at its zenith. look up zenith... 2/26/99

3. *I will also sit on the mount of the congregation.* Notice, Lucifer doesn't want to leave church and backslide. Worldly things, drugs, alcohol and all that mess aren't his Number One attraction. It's church and church business.

4. *I will ascend above the heights of the clouds.* Still power surging...   → Answering To No one...

No more submission. →

No more boss.   ↗

No more checks and balances.

5. *I will be like the Most High.* Sorry Pal. Not!

Lucifer's undoing was his not being satisfied with the anointing and calling on his life. That goes for many dissatisfied ministers today who want more than God is willing to give.

Perceived Injury

David Sumrall, a friend of mine who pastors a great church in Manila, made an interesting observation about the fall of Lucifer. Was Lucifer aware of coming man—God's newest and greatest creation? What would man do for God that the angels couldn't do? Praise Him more? Serve Him better? Fill a need the angels couldn't fill? Would they eventually be replaced?

Perhaps Lucifer got his feelings hurt and felt unappreciated. Maybe he started listening to the praises of other angels in his trading (trafficking). "Lucifer, you're so good, so beautiful, so gifted, so unique and wise, you must be something special!"

Could it be that one day long ago Lucifer shared with other angels he fellowshiped with how man was going to replace them? "God doesn't love us or need us anymore. We used to be important, but no longer. He grows weary of us. If I was your Lord, I'd never let anything come between us. Never. If I was God, you'd always be Number One in my book."

Perceived injury is a hurt based on an opinion or an assumption, not on a fact. Lucifer never asked God; he just assumed what God had in mind.

After one Sunday morning service I was walking through the church sanctuary with a guest speaker. A sister passed by and said, "Hello Pastor." I didn't hear her so naturally, being engrossed in conversation, I did not stop to chat. She got her feelings hurt. On the way home from church the devil whispered to her, "He doesn't care about you. You're just a number, an offering, a warm body to preach to. He's more interested in big shot preachers. See, big churches *are* impersonal and cold."

For six months this woman backslid until one day God shook her up. "He didn't hear you," she kept hearing one morning. "He didn't hear you."

As this sister shared somewhat sheepishly with me what had happened, I felt so sorry for her; yet it made me realize how easy it is for people to perceive and believe things that aren't true.

I wonder how many of the fallen angels wish they had never listened to Lucifer. Hurt feelings can lead to many bad decisions. Cities are full of former church members, people who once were turned-on big time for God, but got their feelings injured and now they're bitter, anti-church, critical and in danger of eternal judgment.

Years ago when I brought a new assistant minister on staff, one of my pastors hit the roof. He saw it as a threat to the little kingdom he had carved out for himself. He eventually left to start his own church a few miles away. In every sermon he took pot shots at us, but I kept my mouth closed. God has His ways. Within six months the group folded, and to this day the man is out of the ministry and the people he convinced to follow him have backslidden.

The spirit of Lucifer is alive and active!

Remember these three P's:
Proximity—Close to the top.
Pride—I'm something special.

Perceived Injury—How dare he do that to me?

The antidote is found in Philippians 2:5-11:

*Let this mind be in you which was also in
Christ Jesus, who, being in the form of God, did
not consider it robbery to be equal with God, but
made Himself of no reputation, taking the form of
a bondservant, and coming in the likeness of men.
And being found in appearance as a man, He
humbled Himself and became obedient to the point
of death, even the death of the cross.*

*Therefore God also has highly exalted Him and
given Him the name which is above every name,
that at the name of Jesus every knee should bow,
of those in heaven, and of those on earth, and of
those under the earth, and that every tongue
should confess that Jesus Christ is Lord, to the
glory of God the Father.*

Chapter 4

JEZEBEL—
QUEEN OF SORROWS

And to the angel of the church in Thyatira write, "These things says the Son of God, who has eyes like a flame of fire, and His feet like fine brass: I know your works, love, service, faith, and your patience; and as for your works, the last are more than the first.

"Nevertheless I have a few things against you, because you allow that woman Jezebel, who calls herself a prophetess, to teach and seduce My servants to commit sexual immorality and eat things sacrificed to idols. And I gave her time to repent of her sexual immorality, and she did not repent. Indeed I will cast her into a sickbed, and those who commit adultery with her into great tribulation, unless they repent of their deeds. I will kill her children with death, and all the churches shall know that I am He who searches the minds and hearts. And I will give to each one of you according to your works."

Now to you I say, and to the rest in Thyatira, as many as do not have this doctrine, who have not known the depths of Satan, as they say, I will put on you no other burden. But hold fast what you have till I come. And he who overcomes, and keeps My works until the end, to him I will give power over the nations.

Revelation 2:18-26

The Jezebel spirit usually operates through women who push themselves off as prophetic. Deep women. Deeper than the pastor. Deeper than God. Jesus calls their insight into spiritual things, "the depths of Satan." (verse 24)

Remember, Jezebel means, "Where is Baal?" The Jezebel spirit is a seeking spirit, always looking for something new. Some new doctrine. The Jezebel spirit uses witchcraft, control, manipulation, sex, religion, rumor spreading, gossip, false prophecies, etc.

This spirit lies at the drop of a hat, digs up one's past, seems overly concerned with leadership in the church, hates male authority, is extremely nosy, bears false witness and loves power. The woman under this spirit's control wants authority but on her terms only. She usually has a cultic following of dysfunctional women and weak wimpy men. She prays a lot, especially for the pastor and his wife, but her prayers are condescending. "Please God, show our little pastor the things you're showing us. Lead him into deeper truth like you have us."

She puts herself above the true leadership of the church. Her doctrine is divisive, not building. She will give words out such as "divorce him," "leave the church," "give me your tithe."

One interesting definition of Jezebel is "inability to cohabitate." If she's married, she wears the pants. It's also common for Jezebels to be unclean sexually. Many, once discovered, prove to be lesbians, adulterers or involved in some kind of sexual uncleanness.

Religious spirits and unclean spirits work hand in hand. Try to bring a word of correction to a Jezebel and

"Katy bar the gate." You've got a hell cat on your hands. Out of the abundance of the heart the mouth speaks. Push her button and blast off.

If repentance isn't in the picture, the only cure is getting her out of the church and marking her from the pulpit. Pastors who hesitate to do so always lose more in the end. There is no détente with these spirits.

The Jezebel spirit places high demands on her followers and you had better live up to them. It's a form of spiritual abuse glossed over and called discipleship.

I have found that most Jezebels come from a dysfunctional background. Unhappy as children, as a mother or wife, they try to gain control by controlling others. The thing they hated most growing up, they end up becoming.

Jezebels will use legitimate means to gain an advantage—Scripture, fasting, prayers, giving, helping out. All good qualities in any healthy Christian walk, but not if there's a hidden agenda or another motive.

The Jezebel spirit has little compassion in dealing with other people's problems.

"Pray more!"

"Where is your faith?"

"If you knew how to do spiritual warfare, you'd not be in this mess."

"Grow up, you big baby."

"Get the sin out of your life and it'll be okay."

Short, curt answers laced with hostility and intolerance is the norm when this spirit is in operation.

Let me borrow a passage from the book, *The Subtle Power of Spiritual Abuse*, by Johnson and VanVonderen.

Three main factors operate in a spiritually abusive system that comprise the "soil" out of which scriptural abuse can grow. They are: mindset, motive, and method. A look at each of these will help you understand how they create an environment where people are scripturally abused.

The first factor is the mindset people have about themselves and Scripture. In a spiritually abusive system, the mindset of the people is that they have little or no capacity to discern God's Word themselves. Their view of Scripture is that of a book of rules, designed to cause behaviors that are pleasing to God, or designed to elicit a desired response from God. In other words, for them, the Bible is not a book that guides us into character transformation so we can be transformed into the likeness of Christ; it is a book about "techniques" for performing right so that we can get corresponding blessing out of God. Spirituality is replaced by manipulation.

As a result, these people view their leaders as those who have the last word on the meaning and purpose of God's Word because the leaders have (or say they have) success at doing and receiving. The mindset of the leaders—about themselves, Scripture, and their followers—is that they have "broken through" to some higher level of spiritual achievement, so they have "earned" the right to lead.

Please note that it is the "achievement" of the leaders that sets the performance standard of the flock. In some settings, it may be evangelizing or witnessing, or discipling young Christians, or claiming victories by faith, or starting home cell groups—whatever the personality of the leadership dictates. In other words, doing more of the prescribed behavior is the goal, not inner transformation into the likeness of Jesus. Those who do more of that behavior are rewarded; those who don't are ignored or counseled to do so; and those who are hurting are told that it is the answer to most or all of their maladies. This leads to the second factor.

In a spiritually abusive system, leaders "power posture" through the use of Scripture. The motive is to cause religious performance on the part of the people in order to meet the needs of the leaders, to "prove" that they and their theology are right. Again, the motive is not to "feed" the souls of the flock, nor to assist God in achieving whatever He wants in a person's life.

In addition to burning people out, pressuring people to "live up to" Scripture leads to a distorted perception of God. He becomes one who is created in the image of the leaders. This is not about helping people gain a deeper understanding of God through the Word, in all its multi-faceted beauty. In fact, a deeper understanding of Scripture on the part of the people would probably expose the whole abusive situation.

The third factor is the method used to study and apply the truth of Scripture. In a spiritually abusive system, Scripture is employed to prove or to bolster the agenda of the person using it. This is called "proof-texting." Proof-texting occurs when someone has a point he wants to prove. So he finds a verse to do so, even if it means stretching or ignoring the original issue about which the verse was written or the context in which the verse is found.

Because this is the method the leaders use, it is the method the followers learn to use. Consequently, there is little if any opportunity to become capable of "rightly dividing the word of truth." (Excerpts from *The Subtle Power of Spiritual Abuse,* by David Johnson and Jeff VanVonderen, Bethany House Publishers, 1991, pp. 82-83.)

Let's look at the historical "Queen of the Sidonians" and see if we can glean a little more information about her modus operandi.

Chapter 5

JEZEBEL—
QUEEN OF DEATH

In the thirty-eighth year of Asa king of Judah, Ahab the son of Omri became king over Israel; and Ahab the son of Omri reigned over Israel in Samaria twenty-two years. Now Ahab the son of Omri did evil in the sight of the Lord, more than all who were before him.

And it came to pass, as though it had been a trivial thing for him to walk in the sins of Jeroboam the son of Nebat, that he took as wife Jezebel the daughter of Ethbaal, king of the Sidonians; and he went and served Baal and worshiped him. Then he set up an altar for Baal in the temple of Baal, which he had built in Samaria. And Ahab made a wooden image.

Ahab did more to provoke the Lord God of Israel to anger than all the kings of Israel who were before him.

I Kings 16:29-33

Ahab represents just how bad off and far from God Israel was. Ahab stands unprecedented in his corruption, profane life and rule more than any other king in all of Israel's history. Prompted by his wife Jezebel he became the most dangerous earthly enemy of God—more than all before him. A covenant man by circumcision, he totally ignored the ways of David and other righteous leaders, and chose his own destiny, religion and pagan wife.

But when it's the darkest, the Lord sends bright lights to show the way. Enter Elijah, the Tishbite. As one author wrote, "Where there's an Ahab, you'll find an Elijah."

Of all the bad decisions Ahab made, his choice for a mate stands out as the worst by far.

Jezebel, the daughter of Ethbaal

Ethbaal—meaning *"with Baal"* or according to the historian Josephus, "With him is Baal." Ethbaal was a high priest of Astarte who gained the throne by assassinating Pheles. His character was passed on to his daughter Jezebel who also was a priestess or minister to her gods Baal and Astarte.

Historians inform us that she was the great aunt of Pygmalion and Dido. Her religious zeal was fierce, determined and greatly devout. As queen, her influence over Ahab, a weak leader, will be looked at in much detail.

I think it's important to note that the figure of Astarte or Ashtoreth, the Canaanite deity, was in the shape of a goat, and the form of worship to this idol was very abominable.

Interesting, today we still have to discern between sheep, goats and wolves. Sheep and wolves are fairly easy to discern, but those goats can fool you. They look somewhat like sheep, sound a little like them, but a closer look tells you—not so.

When Jezebel surfaces and tries a power play, God steps in and takes control. Revivals spring out of great persecution. We are all somewhat familiar with the sequence of events recorded in I Kings 18. The shoot-out at the Mount Carmel OK Corral. God is still the fastest gun around and Jezebel's staff is fired permanently. What a blow to her religion. God's supreme sovereign power was undeniable. Let God be God! Choose you this day whom you will serve! Don't you love it? Out of a hopeless condition comes glory, but is Jezebel convinced or converted? No way.

> *And Ahab told Jezebel all that Elijah had done, also how he had executed all the prophets with the sword. Then Jezebel sent a messenger to Elijah, saying, "So let the gods do to me, and more also, if I do not make your life as the life of one of them by tomorrow about this time." And when he saw that, he arose and ran for his life, and went to Beersheba, which belongs to Judah, and left his servant there. But he himself went a day's journey into the wilderness, and came and sat down under a broom tree. And he prayed that he might die, and said, "It is enough! Now, Lord, take my life, for I am no better than my fathers!"*
>
> *Then as he lay and slept under a broom tree, suddenly an angel touched him, and said to him, "Arise and eat." Then he looked, and there by his head was a cake baked on coals and a jar of water. So he ate and drank, and lay down again. And the angel of the Lord came back the second time, and touched him, and said, "Arise and eat, because the journey is too great for you." So he arose, and ate and drank; and he went in the strength of that food forty days and forty nights as far as Horeb, the mountain of God. And there he went into a cave, and spent the night in that place; and behold, the*

*word of the Lord came to him, and He said to him,
"What are you doing here, Elijah?" So he said, "I
have been very zealous for the Lord God of hosts;
for the children of Israel have forsaken Your
covenant, torn down Your altars, and killed Your
prophets with the sword. I alone am left; and they
seek to take my life."*
1 Kings 19:1-10

Here is a good place to take note of a few of the
tactics of the Jezebel spirit.

1. *And it came to pass after many days that the
word of the Lord came to Elijah, in the third year,
saying, "Go, present yourself to Ahab, and I will
send rain on the earth." So Elijah went to present
himself to Ahab; and there was a severe famine in
Samaria. And Ahab had called Obadiah, who was in
charge of his house. (Now Obadiah feared the Lord
greatly. For so it was, while Jezebel massacred
the prophets of the Lord, that Obadiah had taken
one hundred prophets and hidden them, fifty to a
cave, and had fed them with bread and water.)*
1 Kings 18:1-4

Jezebels want to kill true prophets or sound doctrine and replace them with false prophets, false teaching and false doctrine.

2. *Then Jezebel sent a messenger to Elijah,
saying, "So let the gods do to me, and more also, if
I do not make your life as the life of one of them
by tomorrow about this time."*
1 Kings 19:2

Jezebel will use intimidation to get a point across,
but notice she doesn't do it face to face but through a
messenger.

3. *And when he saw that, he arose and ran for his life, and went to Beersheba, which belongs to Judah, and left his servant there.*

1 Kings 19:3

Elijah bites the bait. He just brought about one of the greatest revivals in history, personally killed off hundreds of false prophets and now he's running from one woman.

Ministers take note: You are most vulnerable to attack right after a great victory. Keep your guard up. Jezebels want you to run, leave town, quit the ministry or get divorced.

4. *But he himself* (Elijah) *went a day's journey into the wilderness, and came and sat down under a broom tree. And he prayed that he might die, and said, "It is enough! Now, Lord, take my life, for I am no better than my fathers!"*

I Kings 19:3,4

Elijah is suicidal. He runs to the wilderness (desert), leaves his companion (servant), and gets him-self isolated. He starts feeling sorry for himself and wants to end it all. Don't underestimate the power of these spirits.

5. *And there he went into a cave, and spent the night in that place; and behold, the word of the Lord came to him, and He said to him, "What are you doing here, Elijah?"*

1 Kings 19:9

What are you doing here Elijah?

When God starts asking you questions, choose your answers slowly. Pity party is over. Get up and go to it, Man of God.

Chapter 6

DON'T LOSE
YOUR INHERITANCE!

And it came to pass after these things that Naboth the Jezreelite had a vineyard which was in Jezreel, next to the palace of Ahab king of Samaria. So Ahab spoke to Naboth, saying, "Give me your vineyard, that I may have it for a vegetable garden, because it is near, next to my house; and for it I will give you a vineyard better than it. Or, if it seems good to you, I will give you its worth in money." But Naboth said to Ahab, "The Lord forbid that I should give the inheritance of my fathers to you!"

So Ahab went into his house sullen and displeased because of the word which Naboth the Jezreelite had spoken to him; for he had said, "I will not give you the inheritance of my fathers." And he lay down on his bed, and turned away his face, and would eat no food.

But Jezebel his wife came to him, and said to him, "Why is your spirit so sullen that you eat no food?"

1 Kings 21:1-5

Few crimes surpass the one we're about to study. A just man, Naboth, is about to get ripped off and killed simply because he has something Ahab wants.

"My residence is incomplete. I must have this vine-yard at all costs." Lust is desire out of control. Naboth recoiled at the idea. The money was not the issue. The land of his fathers was precious to him; an inheritance handed down through generation after generation.

Ahab becomes pitiful and childish. He sulks in his palace and whines to his pagan queen. Her handling of the situation gives us more insight into just how scheming this spirit is.

> *He* (Ahab) *said to her, "Because I spoke to Naboth the Jezreelite, and said to him, 'Give me your vineyard for money; or else, if it pleases you, I will give you another vineyard for it.' And he answered, 'I will not give you my vineyard.'" Then Jezebel his wife said to him, "You now exercise authority over Israel! Arise, eat food, and let your heart be cheerful; I will give you the vineyard of Naboth the Jezreelite."*
> 1 Kings 21:6-7

To Jezebels, authority is simply a means to an end. Justice, right and wrong, morality and integrity mean absolutely nothing. Power without principle is toxic and deadly. Notice this proud, haughty spirit at work. "I will give you the vineyard of Naboth the Jezreelite." She thought her power was unstoppable by God or man.

Look at verse 8:

> *And she wrote letters in Ahab's name, sealed them with his seal, and sent the letters to the elders and the nobles who were dwelling in the city with Naboth.*

40

Jezebels love to write letters in other people's name, especially in God's name. "Pastor, God told me to write you this word of rebuke." Ever get one of those? Or this one—"Pastor, several people have asked me to write you and voice our concerns about our church."

Also, Jezebels are overly concerned with business that's none of theirs. One pastor friend of mine had to throw three Jezebels out of his church for prophesying divorce on several couples. Another term for Jezebel is charismatic witchcraft.

Notice again in verse 8 who the letters are being sent to—elders and nobles. The movers and shakers in leadership. I just had a similar situation in our church with a former staff pastor. He wrote letters and met privately with some of our best people to accuse me of everything except being Adolph Hitler's love child. I've learned something over the years. The guiltiest cry the loudest.

> *She wrote in the letters, saying, "Proclaim a fast, and seat Naboth with high honor among the people."*
>
> 1 Kings 21:9

Jezebels are conniving. They can really lay a trap and use legitimate means to deceive people. Here we see fasting and fellowshiping—a church dinner. Not too bad an idea unless Jezebel's throwing the party.

> *And seat two men, scoundrels, before him to bear witness against him, saying, "You have blasphemed God and the king." Then take him out, and stone him, that he may die.*

So the men of his city, the elders and nobles who were inhabitants of his city, did as Jezebel had sent to them, as it was written in the letters which she had sent to them. They proclaimed a fast, and seated Naboth with high honor among the people. And two men, scoundrels, came in and sat before him; and the scoundrels witnessed against him, against Naboth, in the presence of the people, saying, "Naboth has blasphemed God and the king!" Then they took him outside the city and stoned him with stones, so that he died. Then they sent to Jezebel, saying, "Naboth has been stoned and is dead."

And it came to pass, when Jezebel heard that Naboth had been stoned and was dead, that Jezebel said to Ahab, "Arise, take possession of the vineyard of Naboth the Jezreelite, which he refused to give you for money; for Naboth is not alive, but dead." So it was, when Ahab heard that Naboth was dead, that Ahab got up and went down to take possession of the vineyard of Naboth the Jezreelite.

1 Kings 21:10-16

A good man is discredited, lied about and done in by an insidious plot, but God is still God and takes note of this grievous wrong.

Then the word of the Lord came to Elijah the Tishbite, saying, "Arise, go down to meet Ahab king of Israel, who lives in Samaria. There he is, in the vineyard of Naboth, where he has gone down to take possession of it. You shall speak to him, saying, 'Thus says the Lord: "Have you murdered and also taken possession?"' And you shall speak to him, saying, 'Thus says the Lord: "In the place where dogs licked the blood of Naboth, dogs shall lick your blood, even yours."'"

1 Kings 21:17-19

Also note verse 23:

> *And concerning Jezebel the Lord also spoke, saying, "The dogs shall eat Jezebel by the wall of Jezreel."*

Jezebels never, NEVER succeed! Their victories are short lived and eternity is a long, long time to suffer.

Chapter 7

THE RISE AND FALL
OF JEZEBEL

And Elisha the prophet called one of the sons of the prophets, and said to him, "Get yourself ready, take this flask of oil in your hand, and go to Ramoth Gilead. Now when you arrive at that place, look there for Jehu the son of Jehoshaphat, the son of Nimshi, and go in and make him rise up from among his associates, and take him to an inner room. Then take the flask of oil, and pour it on his head, and say, 'Thus says the Lord: "I have anointed you king over Israel."' Then open the door and flee, and do not delay."

2 Kings 9:1-3

Elijah's gone. Ahab is gone. (Both to different places!) Elisha is the new prophet and Jehu the new king. Ol' Jezzie is still around, but her influence is waning, to say the least.

So the young man, the servant of the prophet, went to Ramoth Gilead. And when he arrived, there were the captains of the army sitting; and he said, "I have a message for you, Commander." Jehu said, "For which one of us?" And he said, "For you, Commander."

Then he arose and went into the house. And he poured the oil on his head, and said to him, "Thus says the Lord God of Israel: 'I have anointed you king over the people of the Lord, over Israel. You shall strike down the house of Ahab your master, that I may avenge the blood of My servants the prophets, and the blood of all the servants of the Lord, at the hand of Jezebel. For the whole house of Ahab shall perish; and I will cut off from Ahab all the males in Israel, both bond and free. So I will make the house of Ahab like the house of Jeroboam the son of Nebat, and like the house of Baasha the son of Ahijah. The dogs shall eat Jezebel on the plot of ground at Jezreel, and there shall be none to bury her.'" And he opened the door and fled.

2 Kings 9:4-10

Jehu is about to do a little house cleaning.

Now it happened, when Joram saw Jehu, that he said, "Is it peace, Jehu?" So he answered, "What peace, as long as the harlotries of your mother Jezebel and her witchcraft are so many?" Then Joram turned around and fled, and said to Ahaziah, "Treachery, Ahaziah!" Now Jehu drew his bow with full strength and shot Jehoram between his arms; and the arrow came out at his heart, and he sank down in his chariot.

2 Kings 9:22-24

Jezebel's children (spiritually speaking) usually go down with her.

Now when Jehu had come to Jezreel, Jezebel heard of it; and she put paint on her eyes and adorned her head, and looked through a window. Then, as Jehu entered at the gate, she said, "Is it peace, Zimri, murderer of your master?" And he looked up at the window, and said, "Who is on my side? Who?" So two or three eunuchs looked out at him. Then he said, "Throw her down." So they threw her down, and some of her blood spattered on the wall and on the horses; and he trampled her underfoot. And when he had gone in, he ate and drank.

Then he said, "Go now, see to this accursed woman, and bury her, for she was a king's daughter." So they went to bury her, but they found no more of her than the skull and the feet and the palms of her hands. Therefore they came back and told him. And he said, "This is the word of the Lord, which He spoke by His servant Elijah the Tishbite, saying, 'On the plot of ground at Jezreel dogs shall eat the flesh of Jezebel; and the corpse of Jezebel shall be as refuse on the surface of the field, in the plot at Jezreel, so that they shall not say, "Here lies Jezebel."'"

2 Kings 9:30-37

Even in her exiting scene she still tries to use her wily ways to gain control. She packs on the makeup and tries to seduce young Jehu. Nothing doing! So she goes to Plan B. A veiled threat, *"Is it peace, Zimri, murderer of your master?"* (verse 31). Again not working. What's left for the queen of problems? Dog food!

Let's review a few things about Jezebel:

- She's very religious.
- She's clever.
- She loves power and authority.
- She goes after leadership.
- She tries to pull people away from their true covering (pastor, church).
- She loves titles (prophetess, deaconess, elder).
- She uses flattery, sex, witchcraft, lies, etc. to gain control.

- She intimidates using other people, letters, telephone, etc.
- She's quick to judge and advise.
- She loves prophetic, faith, charismatic circles.
- She's very patronizing.
- She has a cultic following and claims to be discipling them.
- Her "christianeze" is impeccable.
- She's very inquisitive about the pastor's personal life (spouse, family) and about church business.
- She's hot tempered.
- She's into preserving her little kingdom at all cost.
- She controls her followers with dictatorial tactics.

Now let's move on to see further ways that the Lucifer and Jezebel spirits operated in the Bible.

Chapter 8

ATHALIAH—
DAUGHTER OF JEZEBEL

When Athaliah the mother of Ahaziah saw that her son was dead, she arose and destroyed all the royal heirs. But Jehosheba, the daughter of King Joram, sister of Ahaziah, took Joash the son of Ahaziah, and stole him away from among the king's sons who were being murdered; and they hid him and his nurse in the bedroom, from Athaliah, so that he was not killed. So he was hidden with her in the house of the Lord for six years, while Athaliah reigned over the land.

2 Kings 11:1-3

Athaliah, the daughter of Ahab and Jezebel, was married to Jeboram, son of Jehoshaphat, to cement the alliance between Ahab and Jehoshaphat against the Syrians (see 1 Kings 22:2-4). The curse of her mother was upon her. Athaliah, like Jezebel, had an unlimited ascendancy over her husband, and kept her son Ahaziah tied to her lead strings. She obviously influenced Jehoram to introduce Baal worship into Judah the same way Jezebel stirred Ahab to do likewise in Israel.

After Jehoshaphat died his son Jehoram reigned for only eight years (2 Kings 8:16-18). His son Ahaziah took over and lasted one year. Athaliah, Queen Mother, called by some "The Second Jezebel," panicked. She was about to lose her power and influence. According to law the crown would be passed to one of her grandchildren. The title "Queen Mother" would now go to her daughter-in-law. So without hesitation or remorse, Athaliah went on a killing rampage. All those of Ahab's house whom Jehu the Avenger had left behind (2 Kings 9 & 10) were to be exterminated so she could keep power.

Sin and depravity seem to gain momentum with each generation. As bad as Jezebel was, her daughter seems to have had a double portion. Her fate, like all who openly defy God, was similar to the fate of her mother.

For six years the queen sat on the throne but behind the scenes God was at work (2 Kings 11:3). The remaining "royal heir" was little Joash. Joash was probably an infant when hidden from his murdering grandmother by Athaliah's sister Jehosheba. Jehoiada, the righteous high priest, took the lad and hid him until he was seven.

With a little coaxing the people anointed little Joash to be their king (2 Kings 11:4-12).

Athaliah's days were numbered.

> *Now when Athaliah heard the noise of the escorts and the people, she came to the people in the temple of the Lord. When she looked, there was the king standing by a pillar according to custom; and the leaders and the trumpeters were by the king. All the people of the land were rejoicing and blowing trumpets. So Athaliah tore her clothes and cried out, "Treason! Treason!"*
>
> *And Johoiada the priest commanded the captains of the hundreds, the officers of the army, and said to them, "Take her outside under guard,*

50

and slay with the sword whoever follows her."
For the priest had said, "Do not let her be killed
in the house of the Lord." So they seized her; and
she went by way of the horses' entrance into the
king's house, and there she was killed.

2 Kings 11:13-16

As one reads on, revival came to the land (see verses 17-21).

One day a sister in our church asked me if this story could be connected to the abortion issue of today. Women, and at times their mothers (grandmother of the unborn fetus), plotting a murder to keep the status quo. The wiping out of future children (heirs). A profound thought!

Athaliah didn't want change. She liked her life the way it was and killed to keep it that way. This indeed is something to ponder.

Chapter 9

THE FIRST FAMILY

Now the serpent was more cunning than any beast of the field which the Lord God had made. And he said to the woman, "Has God indeed said, 'You shall not eat of every tree of the garden'?" And the woman said to the serpent, "We may eat the fruit of the trees of the garden; but of the fruit of the tree which is in the midst of the garden, God has said, 'You shall not eat it, nor shall you touch it, lest you die.'"

Then the serpent said to the woman, "You will not surely die. For God knows that in the day you eat of it your eyes will be opened, and you will be like God, knowing good and evil."

So when the woman saw that the tree was good for food, that it was pleasant to the eyes, and a tree desirable to make one wise, she took of its fruit and ate. She also gave to her husband with her, and he ate.

Then the eyes of both of them were opened, and they knew that they were naked; and they sewed fig leaves together and made themselves coverings.

Genesis 3:1-7

Lucifer has been reduced to Satan, the serpent. Notice how he preys. First tactic—isolate, split and divide the man and woman; then go to work on the weaker vessel. As strong as women are in many ways, the temptation to be persuaded is still a weakness that needs constant shoring up. This is not only documented in the Bible but I'm told so by women themselves. One's strength can be an enemy if unchecked. Women, for the most, are listeners, kind, emotional and caring; young girls get talked into things they should avoid.

Again, this is a generalization and if nothing else, Satan knew Eve was the weaker of the two. Here comes the subtle attack.

"Has God indeed said...?" Satan brings into question the Word of God. He's trying to confuse Eve over interpretation. He's not discounting the validity of the Word but, "Eve, did you hear right? Is your husband teaching you right?" The Lucifer spirit is always challenging the teaching of leadership.

Satan is looking for disobedience to God which will lead to obedience to him. The Lucifer spirit questions authority, authenticity and doctrine. This is exactly how Jim Jones and David Koresh led their followers astray. Instead of the Bible being absolute authority, they became the embodiment of truth.

Notice in verse 1 how the devil keys in on the negative and ignores the obvious positive.

> *Has God indeed said, "You shall not eat of every tree of the garden"?*

God had blessed Adam and Eve with all but one tree, and the one was the focal point of Satan's inquiry. Fault finders ignore the massive good that preachers do but look for the one error.

Some authors and radio programs make a living looking for error. They believe they have the anointing to correct others! I've heard them referred to as heretic hunters. I think the Pharisees had the corner on that market, but that fault-finding spirit is also alive and well today.

Chapter 10

CAIN AND ABEL

Now Adam knew Eve his wife, and she conceived and bore Cain, and said, "I have acquired a man from the Lord." Then she bore again, this time his brother Abel. Now Abel was a keeper of sheep, but Cain was a tiller of the ground. And in the process of time it came to pass that Cain brought an offering of the fruit of the ground to the Lord. Abel also brought of the firstborn of his flock and of their fat. And the Lord respected Abel and his offering, but He did not respect Cain and his offering. And Cain was very angry and his countenance fell.

So the Lord said to Cain, "Why are you angry? And why has your countenance fallen? If you do well, will you not be accepted? And if you do not do well, sin lies at the door. And its desire is for you, but you should rule over it."

Now Cain talked with Abel his brother; and it came to pass, when they were in the field, that Cain rose up against Abel his brother and killed him. Then the Lord said to Cain, "Where is Abel your brother?" He said, "I do not know. Am I my brother's keeper?" And He said, "What have you done? The voice of your brother's blood cries out to Me from the ground. So now you are cursed from the earth, which has opened its mouth to receive your brother's blood from your hand. When you till the ground, it shall no longer yield its strength to you. A fugitive and a vagabond you shall be on the earth."

And Cain said to the Lord, "My punishment is greater than I can bear! Surely You have driven me out this day from the face of the ground; I shall be hidden from Your face; I shall be a

fugitive and a vagabond on the earth, and it will happen that anyone who finds me will kill me."
Genesis 4:1-14

Cain is angry, perhaps jealous of his younger brother. Both are in church you could say. Both are worshipers and givers but Cain's lukewarm approach is rejected by God.

God tries to help Cain but rage is in his heart. His jealousy leads him to murder and then when caught he pleads for his wretched life. This reminds me of murderers on death row who rant and rave of how cruel capital punishment is, but forget why they're there in the first place!

Today we see this jealous spirit operating way too much in our churches. Want to get real unpopular pastor? Start having thousands show up on Sunday and see how other pastors react. You're their friend...until you outgrow them. Then you're in it for the bucks, or you must be carnal to attract those kinds or...well, the list is unlimited. They won't take a gun and shoot you, but they'll have a smoking tongue. More character assassinations have taken place in church circles than any other place, based upon this spirit.

Make no friendship with an angry man, and with a furious man do not go, lest you learn his ways and set a snare for your soul.
Proverbs 22:24

Chapter 11

NOAH EXPOSED!

Now the sons of Noah who went out of the ark were Shem, Ham, and Japheth. And Ham was the father of Canaan. These three were the sons of Noah, and from these the whole earth was populated.

And Noah began to be a farmer, and he planted a vineyard. Then he drank of the wine and was drunk, and became uncovered in his tent. And Ham, the father of Canaan, saw the nakedness of his father, and told his two brothers outside. But Shem and Japheth took a garment, laid it on both their shoulders, and went backward and covered the nakedness of their father. Their faces were turned away, and they did not see their father's nakedness. So Noah awoke from his wine, and knew what his younger son had done to him. Then he said: "Cursed be Canaan; a servant of servants he shall be to his brethren."

Genesis 9:18-25

L et's not dance around the issue. Noah got fallen down naked drunk. This is sin in everybody's book. The making or even tasting of his product was acceptable in God's sight, but what Noah did leaves moderation by a mile. Here's a test on how we handle people's mistakes who are above us. Dad, mom, pastor, famous evangelist or boss at work. Someone over us genetically, spiritually or by election. The flesh loves to pull folks down to our level. It justifies our position, especially if we're dissatisfied and looking for advancement. Quick advancement!

Noah's uncovering uncovers more than just his physical nakedness. It exposes flaws in the character of Ham and Canaan. Over and over again the Bible commands us to cover one another's sins. But the world (church world) is full of mean-spirited people who will not rest until their personal judgment is meted out.

Most of us wrestle with this temptation. We are told not to repeat things we hear even about our enemies, let alone friends or especially our parents. Ham tells his two brothers what he saw which is an obvious violation of a natural law, let alone a spiritual one (see verse 22).

The old saying "loose lips sink ships" fits well here. The ship that sunk was the one Canaan was riding on. Why Ham wasn't cursed is much debated, but to have your son cursed is enough heartbreak. What Ham and Canaan saw was true. What they said was true.

One can repeat truth and still be cursed. How we handle truth is constantly under heavenly surveillance. Noah's merciful sons guarded their eyes from sin and covered their father's nakedness. There is a blessing in covering and a curse in exposing.

All sin needs to be dealt with, but how it's dealt with is the key. Sometimes we think God is far too lenient with others and way too hard on us.

Chapter 12

MOSES
AND HIS CRITICS

Then Miriam and Aaron spoke against Moses because of the Ethiopian woman whom he had married; for he had married an Ethiopian woman. So they said, "Has the Lord indeed spoken only through Moses? Has He not spoken through us also?" And the Lord heard it. (Now the man Moses was very humble, more than all men who were on the face of the earth.)

Suddenly the Lord said to Moses, Aaron, and Miriam, "Come out, you three, to the tabernacle of meeting!" So the three came out. Then the Lord came down in the pillar of cloud and stood in the door of the tabernacle, and called Aaron and Miriam. And they both went forward.

Then He said, "Hear now My words: If there is a prophet among you, I, the Lord, make Myself known to him in a vision; I speak to him in a dream. Not so with My servant Moses; He is faithful in all My house. I speak with him face to face, even plainly, and not in dark sayings; and he sees the form of the Lord. Why then were you not afraid to speak against My servant Moses?"

So the anger of the Lord was aroused against them, and He departed. And when the cloud departed from above the tabernacle, suddenly Miriam became leprous, as white as snow. Then Aaron turned toward Miriam, and there she was, a leper.

Numbers 12:1-10

Remember, these spirits work through those who are closest to us. Family, best friends, close associates. Here Moses is being attacked by his sister and brother.

The premise for this power play was Moses' choice for a wife. What business was it of theirs anyway? The old plurality of leadership issue surfaces once again. "Moses has too much power. He needs our help. Hey, God uses us too!"

Recently an elder wanted a real vote and wanted me to add him to the Corporate Board. He assured me that it was for my good and he only had the church's interest at stake. I asked, "Why should I change a procedure that was working fine?" With our advisory elders we discuss all important church issues and pray about each one before we move. Voting is unscriptural and elders can kill a church more quickly than anything else if given power God never intended them to have. Needless to say that elder left once he realized he wasn't going to change my mind.

Amazing, Jubilee is one of the largest congregations in town, giving hundreds of thousands of dollars to missions, converting hundreds and thousands each year here in the San Francisco Bay Area and this guy wants change. No, he wanted Power! Aaron and Miriam want an equal vote or you could say a little prophet-sharing. God wasn't about to alter His ways to please a couple of relatives.

Verse 9 tells us the Lord is angered when we try to usurp authority that is not ours, and with rebellion comes pay day! Miriam is turned into a leper. Lepers were considered cursed by God and unclean. No physical ailment befell Aaron which could mean that Miriam was the force behind the mutiny. Moses intercedes for her and God responds.

> *So Aaron said to Moses, "Oh, my lord! Please do not lay this sin on us, in which we have done foolishly and in which we have sinned. Please do not let her be as one dead, whose flesh is half consumed when he comes out of his mother's womb!" So Moses cried out to the Lord, saying, "Please heal her, O God, I pray!"*
> *Then the Lord said to Moses, "If her father had but spit in her face, would she not be shamed seven days? Let her be shut out of the camp seven days, and afterward she may be received again." So Miriam was shut out of the camp seven days, and the people did not journey till Miriam was brought in again. And afterward the people moved from Hazeroth and camped in the Wilderness of Paran.* Numbers 12:11-16

The redemptive side to this story is that Aaron and Miriam went on to greatness. Both repented and were used by God. There is hope. Things will change if you're having a family feud at church, providing there is genuine repentance before God and one another.

Chapter 13

KORAH

Now Korah the son of Izhar, the son of Kohath, the son of Levi, with Dathan and Abiram the sons of Eliab, and On the son of Peleth, sons of Reuben, took men; and they rose up before Moses with some of the children of Israel, two hundred and fifty leaders of the congregation, representatives of the congregation, men of renown. They gathered together against Moses and Aaron, and said to them, "You take too much upon yourselves, for all the congregation is holy, every one of them, and the Lord is among them. Why then do you exalt yourselves above the assembly of the Lord?" So when Moses heard it, he fell on his face.

Numbers 16:1-4

This insurrection against Moses is a little more than just a family spat. Korah has got himself a crowd. Korah, like many, mistook Moses' position as one of self exaltation. Moses was Moses by the grace of God and for no other reason. Now some of what Korah said is true. All are holy, but not all callings are equal. There's even submission in the Trinity. Father, Son, Holy Ghost. All one. All holy. Yet we see a divine pecking order, if you will. The Father says it, Jesus does it, and the Holy Spirit reveals it.

We see again the humility of Moses in verse 4. He doesn't debate, defend or counter attack. God gives grace to the humble but resists the proud. (James 4:6)

The Lord tells Moses what to do to quench this hostility. Note Numbers 16:5-16:

> *And he* (Moses) *spoke to Korah and all his company, saying, "Tomorrow morning the Lord will show who is His and who is holy, and will cause him to come near to Him. That one whom He chooses He will cause to come near to Him. Do this: Take censers, Korah and all your company; put fire in them and put incense in them before the Lord tomorrow, and it shall be that the man whom the Lord chooses is the holy one. You take too much upon yourselves, you sons of Levi!"*
>
> *Then Moses said to Korah, "Hear now, you sons of Levi: Is it a small thing to you that the God of Israel has separated you from the congregation of Israel, to bring you near to Himself, to do the work of the tabernacle of the Lord, and to stand before the congregation to serve them; and that He has brought you near to Himself, you and all your brethren, the sons of Levi, with you? And are you seeking the priesthood also? Therefore you and all your company are gathered together against the Lord. And what is Aaron that you complain against him?"*
>
> *And Moses sent to call Dathan and Abiram the sons of Eliab, but they said, "We will not come up! Is it a small thing that you have brought us up out of a land flowing with milk and honey, to kill us in the wilderness, that you should keep acting like a prince over us? Moreover you have not brought us into a land flowing with milk and honey, nor given us inheritance of fields and vineyards. Will you put out the eyes of these men? We will not come up!"*

66

> *Then Moses was very angry, and said to the Lord, "Do not respect their offering. I have not taken one donkey from them, nor have I hurt one of them." And Moses said to Korah, "Tomorrow, you and all your company be present before the Lord—you and they, as well as Aaron."*

Moses shows his leadership ability. You can be humble, meek and strong all at the same time. I'm one of the easiest people to work for and get along with, friendly as a golden retriever. But cross me or rebel and you're gone in a heart beat.

As we read on, it still blows my mind that Korah and his followers actually thought God would honor their rebellion. Moses continues speaking to Korah:

> *Let each take his censer and put incense in it, and each of you bring his censer before the Lord, two hundred and fifty censers; both you and Aaron, each with his censer." So every man took his censer, put fire in it, laid incense on it, and stood at the door of the tabernacle of meeting with Moses and Aaron.   And Korah gathered all the congregation against them at the door of the tabernacle of meeting. Then the glory of the Lord appeared to all the congregation.*
>
> *And the Lord spoke to Moses and Aaron, saying, "Separate yourselves from among this congregation, that I may consume them in a moment." Then they fell on their faces, and said, "O God, the God of the spirits of all flesh, shall one man sin, and You be angry with all the congregation?" So the Lord spoke to Moses, saying, "Speak to the congregation, saying, 'Get away from the tents of Korah, Dathan, and Abiram.'"*

Then Moses rose and went to Dathan and Abiram, and the elders of Israel followed him. And he spoke to the congregation, saying, "Depart now from the tents of these wicked men! Touch nothing of theirs lest you be consumed in all their sins." So they got away from around the tents of Korah, Dathan, and Abiram; and Dathan and Abiram came out and stood at the door of their tents, with their wives, their sons, and their little children.

And Moses said: "By this you shall know that the Lord has sent me to do all these works, for I have not done them of my own will. If these men die naturally like all men, or if they are visited by the common fate of all men, then the Lord has not sent me. But if the Lord creates a new thing, and the earth opens its mouth and swallows them up with all that belongs to them, and they go down alive into the pit, then you will understand that these men have rejected the Lord."

Now it came to pass, as he finished speaking all these words, that the ground split apart under them, and the earth opened its mouth and swallowed them up, with their households and all the men with Korah, with all their goods. So they and all those with them went down alive into the pit; the earth closed over them, and they perished from among the assembly.

Numbers 16:17-33

How many churches have you seen prosper that began out of a split or rebellion? Not one! You cannot show me a work accursed of God that is flourishing. God never sanctions a split. Sure, Moses made mistakes. He was very human. Aaron, Miriam and Korah saw his errors as weakness and wanted to take advantage of them, but God has a different scorecard than man.

Chapter 14

JOSHUA AND ACHAN

So the Lord said to Joshua: "Get up! Why do you lie thus on your face? Israel has sinned, and they have also transgressed My covenant which I com-manded them. For they have even taken some of the accursed things, and have both stolen and deceived; and they have also put it among their own stuff. Therefore the children of Israel could not stand before their enemies, but turned their backs before their enemies, because they have become doomed to destruction. Neither will I be with you anymore, unless you destroy the accursed from among you. Get up, sanctify the people, and say, "Sanctify yourselves for tomorrow, because thus says the Lord God of Israel: 'There is an accursed thing in your midst, O Israel; you cannot stand before your enemies until you take away the accursed thing from among you.'"

Joshua 7:10-13

Joshua had big sandals to fill. As the replacement for Moses he was under tremendous pressure but so far all is well. The Jordan parted, Jericho is taken and now little Ai is on the agenda. What could possibly go wrong? We're on a roll. Don't have time to pray and seek God's help. Just do it! But all is not well, Ai is not taken and many Hebrews are killed. Joshua is confused.

> *And Joshua said, "Alas, Lord God, why have You brought this people over the Jordan at all—to deliver us into the hand of the Amorites, to destroy us? Oh, that we had been content, and dwelt on the other side of the Jordan! O Lord, what shall I say when Israel turns its back before its enemies? For the Canaanites and all the inhabitants of the land will hear it, and surround us, and cut off our name from the earth. Then what will You do for Your great name?"*
>
> Joshua 7:7-9

God answers Joshua's prayer in essence this way: "You've got a bad egg on the payroll. His sin is your sin. One of your staff has disobeyed me and is in it for the bucks."

> *"Then it shall be that he who is taken with the accursed thing shall be burned with fire, he and all that he has, because he has transgressed the covenant of the Lord, and because he has done a disgraceful thing in Israel."*
>
> *So Joshua rose early in the morning and brought Israel by their tribes, and the tribe of Judah was taken. He brought the clan of Judah, and he took the family of the Zarhites; and he brought the family of the Zarhites man by man, and Zabdi was taken. Then he brought his household man by man, and Achan the son of Carmi, the son of Zabdi, the son of Zerah, of the tribe of Judah, was taken.*
>
> *Now Joshua said to Achan, "My son, I beg you, give glory to the Lord God of Israel, and make confession to Him, and tell me now what you have done; do not hide it from me."*
>
> *And Achan answered Joshua and said, "Indeed I have sinned against the Lord God of Israel, and*

70

this is what I have done: When I saw among the spoils a beautiful Babylonian garment, two hundred shekels of silver, and a wedge of gold weighing fifty shekels, I coveted them and took them. And there they are, hidden in the earth in the midst of my tent, with the silver under it."
Joshua 7:15-21

One man's sin cost many lives. It's amazing, the ripple affect of iniquity. Starts off as such a little thing; then fans out and touches other lives too.

Years ago I had an Achan bookkeeper. She dipped into the till more than once. We were struggling financially at the time, but eventually like Ai's sin, it was exposed. She confessed and was fired. Personally, I liked her a lot, but she was not honest. Right after our books were put in order, God began to increase our weekly offering by fifteen percent. Make sure you have checks and balances in the handling of church money. Achan is still around.

Chapter 15

DAVID AND SAUL

But the Spirit of the Lord departed from Saul, and a distressing spirit from the Lord troubled him. And Saul's servants said to him, "Surely a distress-ing spirit from God is troubling you. Let our master now command your servants, who are before you, to seek out a man who is a skillful player on the harp. And it shall be that he will play it with his hand when the distressing spirit from God is upon you, and you shall be well."

So Saul said to his servants, "Provide me now a man who can play well, and bring him to me."

Then one of the servants answered and said, "Look, I have seen a son of Jesse the Bethlehemite, who is skillful in playing, a mighty man of valor, a man of war, prudent in speech, and a handsome person; and the Lord is with him."

Therefore Saul sent messengers to Jesse, and said, "Send me your son David, who is with the sheep."

1 Samuel 16:14-19

The story of David and Saul is a classic example of "out with the old and in with the new." I think it fits our teaching but in a little different light. Saul had a lot going for him. A mighty warrior, anointed by God, prophetic and much loved, but Saul was a carnal man. Impetuous at times, his folly conspicuous. Saul began to

73

slip. It got so bad he even consulted a witch for advice, and he was eaten up with jealousy over David.

A series of trials to test Saul's principles were in order. Saul got one "F" after another. When one is proven unfit for service, sooner or later he or she is removed. Saul is on his way out, and how David handled the transition of power is worth noting. The three anointings of David should be looked at.

First Anointing

And Samuel said to Jesse, "Are all the young men here?" Then he said, "There remains yet the youngest, and there he is, keeping the sheep." And Samuel said to Jesse, "Send and bring him. For we will not sit down till he comes here." So he sent and brought him in. Now he was ruddy, with bright eyes, and good-looking. And the Lord said, "Arise, anoint him; for this is the one!" Then Samuel took the horn of oil and anointed him in the midst of his brothers; and the Spirit of the Lord came upon David from that day forward. So Samuel arose and went to Ramah.

1 Samuel 16:11-13

Here I wonder who believed this anointing was real—David? Samuel? His brothers? His father? Perhaps only God knew for sure.

Second Anointing

It happened after this that David inquired of the Lord, saying, "Shall I go up to any of the cities of Judah?" And the Lord said to him, "Go up." David said, "Where shall I go up?" And He said, "To Hebron."

So David went up there, and his two wives also, Ahinoam the Jezreelitess, and Abigail the

74

widow of Nabal the Carmelite. And David brought
up the men who were with him, every man with
his household. So they dwelt in the cities of
Hebron.
Then the men of Judah came, and there they
anointed David king over the house of Judah. And
they told David, saying, "The men of Jabesh Gilead
were the ones who buried Saul."

2 Samuel 2:1-4

After several years of proving himself in battle
(Goliath, Philistines, etc.), David's anointing began to
get recognition. Judah anoints him to be their king.

Third Anointing
*Then all the tribes of Israel came to David at
Hebron and spoke, saying, "Indeed we are your
bone and your flesh. Also, in time past, when Saul
was king over us, you were the one who led Israel
out and brought them in; and the Lord said to you,
'You shall shepherd My people Israel, and be
ruler over Israel.'"*
*Therefore all the elders of Israel came to the
king at Hebron, and King David made a covenant
with them at Hebron before the Lord. And they
anointed David king over Israel.*
*David was thirty years old when he began to
reign, and he reigned forty years.*

2 Samuel 5:1-4

Some seven years later the rest of the tribes
anointed him to be their leader. Could it be that the way
David handled Saul's persecution spoke volumes to the
hearts of the men he would one day lead?
One of the great temptations is to touch the Lord's
anointed, even if we think they deserve it. I wonder why

some stay in their denominations, the way they talk about their leaders.

Another lesson to learn, Pastor, is that your title doesn't automatically make you the pastor of everyone who comes to your church. It took one black sister three years before she could call me Pastor. When she shared why, I understood. God had anointed me years before, but it took our sister a little longer for me to be her pastor because of her past negative experiences. So be patient and don't make false assumptions about your role in people's lives.

Chapter 16

DAVID AND ABSALOM

After this it happened that Absalom provided himself with chariots and horses, and fifty men to run before him. Now Absalom would rise early and stand beside the way to the gate. So it was, whenever anyone who had a lawsuit came to the king for a decision, that Absalom would call to him and say, "What city are you from?" And he would say, "Your servant is from such and such a tribe of Israel."

Then Absalom would say to him, "Look, your case is good and right; but there is no deputy of the king to hear you." Moreover Absalom would say, "Oh, that I were made judge in the land, and everyone who has any suit or cause would come to me; then I would give him justice."

And so it was, whenever anyone came near to bow down to him, that he would put out his hand and take him and kiss him. In this manner Absalom acted toward all Israel who came to the king for judgment. So Absalom stole the hearts of the men of Israel.

2 Samuel 15:1-6

Power-hungry people make their own arrangements. They can't wait for God to open doors. They take matters into their own hands.

Absalom fakes genuine concern for people's problems. Absalom's conspiracy was well thought out.

> *Now it came to pass after forty years that Absalom said to the king, "Please, let me go to Hebron and pay the vow which I made to the Lord. For your servant took a vow while I dwelt at Geshur in Syria, saying, 'If the Lord indeed brings me back to Jerusalem, then I will serve the Lord.'" And the king said to him, "Go in peace." So he arose and went to Hebron.*
>
> *Then Absalom sent spies throughout all the tribes of Israel, saying, "As soon as you hear the sound of the trumpet, then you shall say, 'Absalom reigns in Hebron!'" And with Absalom went two hundred men invited from Jerusalem, and they went along innocently and did not know anything.*
>
> *Then Absalom sent for Ahithophel the Gilonite, David's counselor, from his city–from Giloh–while he offered sacrifices. And the conspiracy grew strong, for the people with Absalom continually increased in number.*
>
> 2 Samuel 15:7-12

Here are the steps Absalom followed to try and gain power:

1. Win over the people by criticizing the king and his administration.
2. Exalt himself as the righteous man of the hour.
3. Go after key leadership in David's camp.

David was blinded to truth by parental love. In the past I have allowed friendships to cloud my better judgment. Absalom was a prince of flattery (perverted praise) and was taking advantage of his father's short-comings. Evil men are quick to seize the moment of opportunity. Yet, God allows only so much before he turns the tide.

> *So the people went out into the field of battle against Israel. And the battle was in the woods of Ephraim. The people of Israel were overthrown there before the servants of David, and a great slaughter of twenty thousand took place there that day. For the battle there was scattered over the face of the whole countryside, and the woods devoured more people that day than the sword devoured.*
>
> *Then Absalom met the servants of David. Absalom rode on a mule. The mule went under the thick boughs of a great terebinth tree, and his head caught in the terebinth; so he was left hanging between heaven and earth. And the mule which was under him went on.*
>
> *Now a certain man saw it and told Joab, and said, "I just saw Absalom hanging in a terebinth tree!" So Joab said to the man who told him, "You just saw him! And why did you not strike him there to the ground? I would have given you ten shekels of silver and a belt."*
>
> *But the man said to Joab, "Though I were to receive a thousand shekels of silver in my hand, I would not raise my hand against the king's son. For in our hearing the king commanded you and Abishai and Ittai, saying, 'Beware lest anyone touch the young man Absalom!' Otherwise I would have dealt falsely against my own life. For there is nothing hidden from the king, and you yourself would have set yourself against me."*
>
> *Then Joab said, "I cannot linger with you." And he took three spears in his hand and thrust them through Absalom's heart, while he was still alive in the midst of the terebinth tree. And ten young men who bore Joab's armor surrounded Absalom, and struck and killed him.*

2 Samuel 18:6-15

Having two fine sons, I cannot imagine the pain David must have gone through. The powers of greed, lust and envy are real and unfortunately can get off on even siblings. God tells us all along that life and blessing are for those who honor mother and father.

Chapter 17

DAVID AND JOAB

J oab is a picture of loyalty to a fault. Loyalty is good but not if it's blind loyalty. Joab was David's right-hand man. A mighty captain of warriors but Joab took matters into his own hands once too often. Loyalty is no replacement for godliness.

At that moment the servants of David and Joab came from a raid and brought much spoil with them. But Abner was not with David in Hebron, for he had sent him away, and he had gone in peace. When Joab and all the troops that were with him had come, they told Joab, saying, "Abner the son of Ner came to the king, and he sent him away, and he has gone in peace."

Then Joab came to the king and said, "What have you done? Look, Abner came to you; why is it that you sent him away, and he has already gone? Surely you realize that Abner the son of Ner came to deceive you, to know your going out and your coming in, and to know all that you are doing." And when Joab had gone from David's presence, he (Joab) sent messengers after Abner, who brought him back from the well of Sirah. But David did not know it.

Now when Abner had returned to Hebron, Joab took him aside in the gate to speak with him privately, and there stabbed him in the stomach, so that he died for the blood of Asahel his brother.

> *Afterward, when David heard it, he said, "My kingdom and I are guiltless before the Lord forever of the blood of Abner the son of Ner. Let it rest on the head of Joab and on all his father's house; and let there never fail to be in the house of Joab one who has a discharge or is a leper, who leans on a staff or falls by the sword, or who lacks bread."*
>
> *So Joab and Abishai his brother killed Abner, because he had killed their brother Asahel at Gibeon in the battle.*
>
> 2 Samuel 3:22-30

According to 2 Samuel 11, Joab was in on the death of Uriah, the Hittite. David had gone into Bathsheba and made her pregnant. Joab obeyed David's ungodly plan.

> *So it was, while Joab besieged the city, that he assigned Uriah to a place where he knew there were valiant men. Then the men of the city came out and fought with Joab. And some of the people of the servants of David fell; and Uriah the Hittite died also. Then Joab sent and told David all the things concerning the war.*
>
> 2 Samuel 11:16-18

Joab saw to it that Absalom, David's own son, was killed. Joab, like some staff members, think they know what's best for the boss. They just do it without considering the outcome.

On David's deathbed, he realized Joab's faults and to his heir apparent, Solomon, he gave this command:

> *"Moreover you know also what Joab the son of Zeruiah did to me, and what he did to the two commanders of the armies of Israel, to Abner the*

son of Ner and Amasa the son of Jether, whom he killed. And he shed the blood of war in peacetime, and put the blood of war on his belt that was around his waist, and on his sandals that were on his feet. Therefore do according to your wisdom, and do not let his gray hair go down to the grave in peace."

1 Kings 2:5-6

Chapter 18

JUDAS

And when He had called His twelve disciples to Him, He gave them power over unclean spirits, to cast them out, and to heal all kinds of sickness and all kinds of disease.

Now the names of the twelve apostles are these: first, Simon, who is called Peter, and Andrew his brother; James the son of Zebedee, and John his brother; Philip and Bartholomew; Thomas and Matthew the tax collector; James the son of Alphaeus, and Lebbaeus, whose surname was Thaddaeus; Simon the Canaanite, and Judas Iscariot, who also betrayed Him.

Matthew 10:1-4

Judas was one of the original apostles. He, like the others, healed, delivered and ministered in power. Even our Lord had a rotten apple on staff. Judas loved money. He was the treasurer of Jesus' ministry.

Then, six days before the Passover, Jesus came to Bethany, where Lazarus was who had been dead, whom He had raised from the dead. There they made Him a supper; and Martha served, but Lazarus was one of those who sat at the table with Him.

Then Mary took a pound of very costly oil of spikenard, anointed the feet of Jesus, and wiped His feet with her hair. And the house was filled with the fragrance of the oil. But one of His disciples, Judas Iscariot, Simon's son, who would betray Him, said, "Why was this fragrant oil not sold for three hundred denarii and given to the poor?" This he said, not that he cared for the poor, but because he was a thief, and had the money box; and he used to take what was put in it.

But Jesus said, "Let her alone; she has kept this for the day of My burial. For the poor you have with you always, but Me you do not have always."

John 12:1-8

Then one of the twelve, called Judas Iscariot, went to the chief priests and said, "What are you willing to give me if I deliver Him to you?" And they counted out to him thirty pieces of silver. So from that time he sought opportunity to betray Him.

Matthew 26:14-16

Now the Feast of Unleavened Bread drew near, which is called Passover. And the chief priests and the scribes sought how they might kill Him, for they feared the people. Then Satan entered Judas, surnamed Iscariot, who was numbered among the twelve. So he went his way and conferred with the chief priests and captains, how he might betray Him to them. And they were glad, and agreed to give him money.

Luke 22:1-5

Many a soul has been sold for the right price. I've seen too many ministries go down because of mismanagement of funds. The Lord has much to say about stewardship. Preachers who are in it for the money don't last. When speakers wants to come to our church, then name their minimum price, I never have them. I live by faith, you live by faith, why can't they? I guess if they had faith and prayed, they wouldn't need a guarantee, would they?

Chapter 19

PAUL—THE
ABANDONED APOSTLE

*Be diligent to come to me quickly; for Demas
has forsaken me, having loved this present world,
and has departed for Thessalonica—Crescens for
Galatia, Titus for Dalmatia. Only Luke is with me.
Get Mark and bring him with you, for he is useful
to me for ministry. And Tychicus I have sent to
Ephesus. Bring the cloak that I left with Carpus at
Troas when you come—and the books, especially
the parchments.*

*Alexander the coppersmith did me much
harm. May the Lord repay him according to his
works. You also must beware of him, for he has
greatly resisted our words. At my first defense no
one stood with me, but all forsook me. May it not
be charged against them.*

2 Timothy 4:9-16

Talk about staff challenges. Paul was either
impossible to work for or Satan sent a lot of problems
his way to stop his assignment. Paul had his way of
dealing with rebels.

*Now I urge you, brethren, note those who
cause divisions and offenses, contrary to the
doctrine which you learned, and avoid them. For
those who are such do not serve our Lord Jesus*

Christ, but their own belly, and by smooth words and flattering speech deceive the hearts of the simple.

For your obedience has become known to all. Therefore I am glad on your behalf; but I want you to be wise in what is good, and simple concerning evil. And the God of peace will crush Satan under your feet shortly. The grace of our Lord Jesus Christ be with you. Amen.

Romans 16:17-20

Don't be afraid to mark people when necessary. Recently a pastor friend asked my advice about a growing problem in his church. A former staff member who couldn't or wouldn't submit was calling members and lying about the pastor. "What should I do?" he inquired. "Mark him next Sunday," I retorted without batting an eye. "Tell the people why he's no longer with the church and what he's up to."

"Gee, I don't know if I can, Dick." "Well, okay then, have a split," I said.

Ministers, we are not in the people business, we're in the God business, and truth is truth. Since when do we have to protect people from truth? What the sheep need is protection from wolves.

Reject a divisive man after the first and second admonition, knowing that such a person is warped and sinning, being self-condemned.

Titus 3:10-11

Cast out the scoffer, and contention will leave; yes, strife and reproach will cease.

Proverbs 22:10

Pastor, I suggest you have every present staff member and future employee read this little book. I don't think I'm going to win any Pulitzer Prize or go hardback with it, but this I do know. If I had this wisdom thirteen years ago, I'd sure have saved myself a lot of hell; but life is good and getting better. Pastoring is the greatest and toughest calling there is and I wouldn't trade it for the whole world.

Chapter 20

A WARNING TO
ELDERS

*Now some of the elders of Israel came to me
and sat before me. And the word of the Lord came
to me, saying, "Son of man, these men have set up
their idols in their hearts and put before them
that which causes them to stumble into iniquity.
Should I let Myself be inquired of at all by them?
Therefore speak to them, and say to them, 'Thus
says the Lord God: "Everyone of the house of Israel
who sets up his idols in his heart, and puts before
him what causes him to stumble into iniquity, and
then comes to the prophet, I the Lord will answer
him who comes, according to the multitude of his
idols."'"*

Ezekiel 14:1-4

*I will set My face against that man and make
him a sign and a proverb, and I will cut him off
from the midst of My people. Then you shall know
that I am the Lord.*

Ezekiel 14:8

Maybe it's only fitting that I should end on a word
of warning to elders. I love elders. They're necessary
working parts in the Body. I personally don't believe in
voting or "boards" but that's me. How you want to use

93

your elders is your business. We have a Corporate Board of five and an Advisory Counsel of several.

My elders are divided into two groups. Executive elders (four) help me in financial matters. Our ministerial elders oversee large ministries and lobby for them at our monthly Pow Wows.

In Ezekiel 14 we see a deadly situation. Elders with their own mindset (idols). They come to church, do all the "church" things and speak "christianeze," yet there is a real problem in their hearts. High places and strongholds! Things demons can take advantage of and deceive, if not destroy.

Notice God's reply to their wanting a "word."

> *Therefore speak to them, and say to them, "Thus says the Lord God: 'Everyone of the house of Israel who sets up his idols in his heart, and puts before him what causes him to stumble into iniquity, and then comes to the prophet, I the Lord will answer him who comes, according to the multitude of his idols.'"*
>
> Ezekiel 14:4

In essence, God is saying, "You want a word from Me? No you don't because I speak the truth. What you want has already been determined by your own desire. Your own object of desire. Your will, not mine."

So the Lord goes on to say, "Okay, you'll get a word, but it'll come from hell and flesh, and you'll think it's from me. You'll tell people it's from me. It may even sound and feel like Me, but it's not."

When some people tell you they heard from God and you know what they heard is absurd, don't think they didn't hear. They heard from a "lord" (Baal) all right, but not from the Lord God.

Now look again at Ezekiel 14:8:

> *I will set My face against that man and make him a sign and a proverb, and I will cut him off from the midst of My people. Then you shall know that I am the Lord.*

Elders beware. God gives grace to the humble but resists the proud.

CONCLUSION

Recently someone faxed me a quotation that went like this: "If life isn't a test, God would have given us more instructions." I have to remind myself constantly that life *is* a test, and I'm being graded daily. Why do I need this? Do I have to go through all this?

Perhaps this is a good place to insert several verses from Hebrews:

> *Therefore we must give the more earnest heed to the things we have heard, lest we drift away. For if the word spoken through angels proved steadfast, and every transgression and disobedience received a just reward, how shall we escape if we neglect so great a salvation, which at the first began to be spoken by the Lord, and was confirmed to us by those who heard Him, God also bearing witness both with signs and wonders, with various miracles, and gifts of the Holy Spirit, according to His own will?*
>
> *For He has not put the world to come, of which we speak, in subjection to angels. But one testified in a certain place, saying:*

"What is man that You are mindful of him, or the son of man that You take care of him? You have made him a little lower than the angels; You have crowned him with glory and honor, and set him over the works of Your hands. You have put all things in subjection under his feet."

For in that He put all in subjection under him, He left nothing that is not put under him. But now we do not yet see all things put under him. But we see Jesus, who was made a little lower than the angels, for the suffering of death crowned with glory and honor, that He, by the grace of God, might taste death for everyone. For it was fitting for Him, for whom are all things and by whom are all things, in bringing many sons to glory to make the captain of their salvation perfect through sufferings.

Hebrews 2:1-10

And I want to add James 1:2-4:

My brethren, count it all joy when you fall into various trials, knowing that the testing of your faith produces patience. But let patience have its perfect work, that you may be perfect and complete, lacking nothing.

I'm on a roll. How about a dose of 1 Peter 1:6-9:

In this you greatly rejoice, though now for a little while, if need be, you have been grieved by various trials, that the genuineness of your faith, being much more precious than gold that perishes, though it is tested by fire, may be found to praise, honor, and glory at the revelation of Jesus Christ, whom having not seen you love.

Though now you do not see Him, yet believing, you rejoice with joy inexpressible and full of glory, receiving the end of your faith–the salvation of your souls.

And lastly, 1 Peter 4:12-16:

Beloved, do not think it strange concerning the fiery trial which is to try you, as though some strange thing happened to you; but rejoice to the extent that you partake of Christ's sufferings, that when His glory is revealed, you may also be glad with exceeding joy.

If you are reproached for the name of Christ, blessed are you, for the Spirit of glory and of God rests upon you. On their part He is blasphemed, but on your part He is glorified.

But let none of you suffer as a murderer, a thief, an evildoer, or as a busybody in other people's mat-ters. Yet if anyone suffers as a Christian, let him not be ashamed, but let him glorify God in this matter.

Obviously you and I aren't the first leaders to feel pressure, persecution, betrayal, loneliness and at times hopelessness. As one ol' farmer once said, "Son, fruit is grown in the valleys, not on the mountain tops."

What are we going to do—quit or perservere? Sit down or press on? Surrender or fight? Hold our own or run? I found my answer. Even after 13 years of going through unspeakable challenges, there isn't anything like ministry. It's rewarding, fun, exciting, exhilarating and adventurous. I get to see the finest people on earth every Sunday, meet new friends and fellow-laborers, travel, evangelize, write, do radio and TV shows and present Jesus at every opportunity. Am I going to let a few Jezzies and Lucifers ruin my good time?

I don't think so!

OTHER BOOKS BY DICK BERNAL

Removing the 'Ites' From Your
Promised Land... $5.95
America Spiritually Mapped..........................$9.95
Questions God Asks..$5.95
Who Is God? What Is Man? $6.95
Curses: What They Are
and How to Break Them $6.95
Come Down Dark Prince.............................. $4.95

COMING SOON!
Lifting Him Up
by Dick Bernal and Ron Kenoly

Available through

Jubilee Christian Center
175 Nortech Parkway • San Jose, CA 95134

(408) 262-0900